Don't get gubbed - how to stay under the bookies radar and bank big long-term matched betting or arbitrage profits!

By Dillon Bleakley

Table of Contents

What path are you on?

The gambling world is massive! And there's lots of us utilising it to make nice tax-free profits. Understandably the bookies don't like paying out to the well-organised people with their systems and their spreadsheets. They want the mugs that'll spaff their earnings up the wall every week! So we're not welcome even though we're not doing anything illegal.

As a result of the bookies not wanting those of us who use; arbitrage betting, matched betting, horse racing systems, or are just damn professionals who know their stuff, they go to great lengths to chuck us out.

Being 'gubbed' is the industry word used for when your account is limited. Or 'getting a gubbing' as I like to say. How your account gets limited can vary. Sometimes they block you from using any promotional offers. Sometimes they limit the maximum bet you can place. Sometimes they just close your account altogether using a polite email. And because the different companies work together you may find one gubbing leads to other gubbings. How charming!

Having done this for many years I feel very proud to have never had a single account gubbed (touch wood!). Maybe you have had one or two accounts gubbed, or maybe you're worried about it. Have no fear, this book is here! Having spent a long time working on this I'm pleased it's paid dividends for me very nicely so far, and it should do for you too.

So the aim is simple. Whether you're new to the industry or a pro who's made money for many years. It doesn't matter. We don't want to get gubbed!

This book is designed for anyone utilising any profitable betting system. Across the internet you'll find forum posts of people saying, "I've been gubbed!" We never want to be that person. Most people don't make the effort to avoid gubbing, and they pay the price. Not us! We want to be making hundreds of pounds per month not just for a short while, but for decades. That's our aim. Let's stay under the bookies radar and bank large profits over the long-term! This book will put you on a nice long profitable path and hopefully if needed you can return to it and stay on the path of profits forever. Don't do these things and you highly risk being on a path that abruptly ends.

Preword

The bookies have entire departments watching their membership base. These people are risk managers, data scientists, and mathematicians. The bookies want punters good for them, not organised people (that's me and you!) that are guaranteed to take money off them over the long-term.

I'm by no means saying you have to do all the things listed in this book, and I'm by no means saying that by not doing them you're 100% guaranteed to get gubbed eventually. You might get lucky. What I'm saying is that despite doing this for many years I've never been gubbed, not once, and make consistently healthy tax-free profits. In this book is my advice, if you don't want to take it then it's fine by me because it won't affect my profits, but it will affect yours. Make the effort and you stand a very good chance of keeping the profits coming in for a very long time!

The blocks of advice in this book are not in order of importance, they're all incredibly important. No matter whether you're betting for a living earning a serious income or using it as a little side hustle to make money online alongside your main job, everything needs to be followed the same by all of us! I'm afraid that means you need to read all of the book! It won't take long, I've tried to keep the whole book to a concise pocket book so you only get the vital information and minimum amounts of fluff. Please don't be alarmed at how short this book is, not every book has to be 400 pages long! Most books are fleshed out with unnecessary fluff so buyers feel like they are getting value for money. The value here is in the quality of the information as you're now going to find out. For the small price you've paid relative to the very long-term profits you can make, I hope you consider this a fantastic investment.

Okay let's get going...

Actually wait, a few key themes first

Before we get stuck in there's a few key themes running through the book so I just want to introduce them to you know so they make sense from the start.

A key theme is 'acting natural', this may sound obvious and dumb but I'm sure as you read the whole book it will make more and more sense and you'll become more aware of your own actions. It's vitally important.

A phrase you'll hear is 'mug bets' which is a type of betting done to make your account look more natural (there's that word again!). There's a page fully about it later on so don't get too worried about it.

There's also some slightly techie stuff to do with tracking and web browsers, don't be overwhelmed by it if you're not very techie. It's important and easy to follow! I've tried to make this book suitable even for dummies because I didn't do well at school so I tend to set myself as the benchmark. If I can follow it, anyone can follow it.

Ultimately the core fundamental theme that runs throughout this book is we're trying not to raise any red flags, You'll see me say that many times, but it's literally the whole point, we're trying not to raise any red flags, so it'll get said many times! Hopefully it's drummed into you by the end.

And one last recommendation. You might want to grab a pen and a piece of paper, or create a document on your computer or smartphone. And keep notes specific to yourself based on what each page says, because they all have a section called *'Your required actions'*. This isn't absolutely critical, you could remember stuff in your noggin. But writing it down may help.

Okay, finally, onto number 1 (remember they're in no particular order).

Limit the number of markets you bet on

Let's get started with a nice easy straight-forward one. I do 85% of my bets on football markets, for my other bets I dabble in a bit of F1, golf, and rugby union. For golf I stick with the big occasions such as the majors. Always focus on specific sports. If you're match betting on absolutely everything including sports you may have minimal knowledge of, like basketball and baseball, it can trigger a signal. Is that really the behaviour of somebody betting for fun? For a few it will be, but not for the vast majority of punters, they bet on only a few types of sports, and the types they like.

When keeping within those markets always limit yourself to certain leagues too. For example when betting on football I stick very heavily with the Premier League and a bit of Championship football too. When the FA cup comes around that can be good for a few mug bets (more on mug bets later!) trying to guess some giant killings that are about to occur. It's good fun and a way to keep your account in good order. Other major events might get a look-in as well, such as the Olympics or the Euros or the Champions League Final, but even then I won't go in heavily on them. £1 or £2 is fine, having fun bets rather than going for a straight-up winner.

Another reason I like these markets is high volume, the bookies will be getting lots of action on them, blending in with that volume is ideal and also means no problems when placing bets on exchanges like Betfair.

Your required actions
Pick the markets you're going to bet on, write them down to guarantee your focus. Don't just have one sport, go for at least two. For horse betting systems you'll want to keep 90% of your bets on the horses as well as maybe having one other sport. Once you've picked your sports be sure to never waiver into other random sports.

Bet on the same team(s) often

This is a great way to make yourself look like a natural punter. If you are betting on football you probably already have a team you support. If not make sure it's a local team or one of the big dawgs like Man Utd or Chelsea. This is something lots of natural punters do quite a bit, meaning it's a great tactic for us to do!

The downside? If doing matched betting it means sometimes the profit we make won't be as good because the odds on our Back and Lay bets are not as close as we would like, or could get on other matches. But if it means making £18.50 instead of £20 I still go for it. It's a small price to pay for a great way to look natural.

Your required actions

Pick a team to bet consistently on, preferably local to you (remember the bookie can see your address) or one of the big teams, bet lots of games they are in whether it's for mug bets or part of your strategy it doesn't matter.

Don't take offers on markets or types of bets you don't place

If you do it's a clear sign you are just out to take every offer. A sure fire way to get restrictions placed on your account! Some websites have accumulator offers which I never take up even if they sound really good. I don't ever bet on accumulators so suddenly placing one to just take up the offer and then not placing any more accumulators after that would be a fairly big red flag. Same goes for horse racing, I don't bet on horses other than when I'm actually at the races in person. Therefore if I see online offers specific to the horses, I leave them well alone.

No matter how tempting they are, don't take up offers just because they're available. If you use the offer, and then never bet on the same market again, you're raising a big red flag against your account.

Your required actions

If this is something you've done in the past then avoid doing it again. Write this tip down, don't forget it and be sure to get in the habit of not taking every offer, only take those in the markets you normally bet on. It's healthy to show the bookies we don't take up every offer.

Take time off when no big events are on in your main sport

This ties in to what I said about focusing on certain markets. When the football season has finished it means a couple of months where I won't bet on any football, unless the Euros or World Cup are on. I don't want to bet on friendlys or random games in foreign countries, I feel that stands a good chance of being a big red flag even if my betting system is showing it will be profitable. It's an even bigger red flag if I continue to profit even though I'm betting on abnormal random stuff I don't normally bet on!

In the quieter times when the markets you bet on aren't in full flow it's ok to leave your accounts alone for days or weeks, or even a couple of months. Safe in the knowledge that when the season kicks off again the bookies offers and the profitable opportunities come in thick and fast and you can have some very profitable months which make up for the reduced profit in previous months. Also remember that if a bookie flags your account for the betting patterns to be monitored by their trading team for a while, it will help that you weren't betting outside of the regular football season as it shows a natural pattern. This could lead to them dropping their monitoring of you.

Once again; remember the behaviour of natural punters. Are they logging in most days anyway? No, it's highly unlikely, if someone is a football bettor they tend to login at weekends and the odd evening to place their bets on the premier league! It will look unnatural logging in everyday anyway, so take a break now and again and don't worry about it.

I also tend to take the opportunity to look closely at my bookie accounts and see how the different ones have gone. If one is up a lot, and has shown a profit every month for continuous months, I'll use the quiet time to place a few mug bets at long odds where I can, it normally ends up being an F1 race or a golf competition. The aim is to make a loss while maintaining the chance of a big win. Why? Because I want to try and avoid their systems triggering the fact I've had 4 winning months on the trot on their website, hopefully a losing month, albeit small, will help me stay under the radar. But if the bet gets super lucky and wins then at least it's a juicy win!

That's why I like to bet on the golf. If I bet on a golfer with long odds and it comes in (which does happen in golf majors!) then it can be a nice win. For example, The Masters in 2021 was won by Hideki Matsuyama, he had pre-competition odds of 60-1! And yet this is a guy who had already played the competition 10 times and only missed the cut once, including 6 finishes inside the top-25. He wasn't some young newbie who'd never played at Augusta before, he was already a known top player. That's the sort of bet I like because it's not in my main market of football, but it's in a secondary market I do bet on, it's a small bet that is highly likely to result in a 'mug bet' loss for me, but if it gets lucky then it's a big win.

Your required actions

When no big events are on for your chosen markets, don't force the situation. Take the opportunity to take a step back and enjoy some of the profits! Maybe even place a few mug bets (like my golf example above) to show small losses on highly profitable sites. If you want to you can leave the laptop turned off and look forward to the profits flowing again in the months ahead.

Only login/bet at social times

By 'social times' I mean evenings and weekends, when most people have finished work. This looks more natural and gives you more chance of blending as a regular punter. Don't even login during the day, only ever be active in the evenings and weekends.

If you have a job or commitments which mean there's no way this is possible then just be sure you are fairly consistent with the times you login so your account activity is consistent. If you bet on the horses then once again be sure to keep it fairly consistent.

Your required actions

Be sure to follow this rule, if you need to write it down then do so, or set a daily alarm or whatever you have to do – just don't forget it!

Place bets just before the event starts

If you do matched betting and plan ahead and are always logging in 3 or 4 days before weekend matches and placing your bets, then it's a pretty big giveaway that you are an organised professional who is clearly researching and planning what you're doing. Avoid this as much as you can, preferably all the time. Placing bets close to the event helps us blend in with the volume and looks more natural because that is what most punters do. It also ensures good volume for when placing exchange bets on sites like Betfair or Smarkets.

Your required actions

If you've been betting well ahead of events then stop it. If you're just starting out then get in the habit from the beginning of placing bets just before the event. I know it's boring to keep repeating this – but write this down in your notes or do whatever you have to do to remember it.

Mimic natural behaviour while logged in

Most casual punters won't just quickly login, place a bet and leave. Often they'll stick around and check different odds, as well as maybe even watch a live stream. They'll also often be logged in as a bet is about to be completed. They're excited to see their balance go up when the winnings go in!

The behaviour of some people betting professionally is to login, place the bets and leave. Then they come back tomorrow to calculate their exact profits. This obviously is not similar behaviour to the natural punter who is understandably keen to check the result of their bets as soon as the events they've bet on have finished. Try and mimic this behaviour.

These days live 'in-play' betting is also very popular with punters. Don't be afraid to mimic natural behaviour on your mug bets (discussed later on) and close them early on while they're in-play to bank some small wins.

Your required actions

Leave your account logged in and spend a bit of time on bookies sites when you've placed the bets or when they are just about to come in. Like I keep saying, always try and mimic natural punters behaviour as much as you can.

Use two devices, one for placing bets and one for web research/info, plus use a VPN

I use my laptop to place all my bets. Apart from placing my bets I don't use it for any kind of research or anything whatsoever to do with betting. In my hand I have an old smartphone and it's on that device I will read blogs and forums and other information. Although for the last few years I've not bothered with them because I have my routines and systems in place and don't need them anymore. But regardless, you should do the same and have a two device setup at all times.

Why is this important? Because of tracking! Companies know far more than you're probably aware of. They have different methods too.

For all your research it's also good to use a VPN for an extra layer of security to hide your IP too. I personally have never paid for a VPN. If you already pay for one then happy days, you're all set. If you don't have one and don't want to pay one for then no problems! Opera is your friend. No not the form of musical theatre, I mean 'Opera', the browser! It's a browser the same as Firefox and Chrome. But it has a built-in VPN you can use for free. You can get it on PC/laptop as well as Android and iOS if you want it on a smartphone. The downside to the free Opera VPN is it only has a couple of locations. In comparison the paid-for VPN's have hundreds. But I've always used Opera no problem! Don't just take my word for it, please be sure to do your own research to learn about the Opera browser before downloading it. Be sure to only use the VPN when researching, and not while on actual gambling websites, otherwise they'll see your IP as being in a completely different country and it's highly probable they will start investigating your account at that point.

If you use Apple devices, such as the iPhone, be aware of IDFA. It stands for (Identifier for Advertisers). Imagine you're using the Facebook app and see an advert for a clothing company. Then a couple of weeks later you're shopping for new clothes and you buy from that same clothing company that previously showed you an advert. When you checkout on the clothing company app it will tell Facebook (without you knowing) that you've made a purchase and it will know you previously saw an advert for that company on Facebook. Even though the two events weren't connected! Pretty spooky huh. That's how much big brother is watching and just how crazy the personal data situation is. Thankfully as of iOS14 Apple have added a feature that allows you to turn off IDFA. It's worth doing! Hopefully this gives an insight into how tracking is done, and there's no reason to believe gambling companies don't go to such lengths with tracking users too.

One simple method that some websites also use to understand their traffic is the ability to see the referrer of their visitor. Meaning the website the person was on before they visited their website can be known. For example, if you're on a matched betting blog, click a link and land on the bookies website and sign up, they might be able to see you came from a matched betting blog. You definitely don't want this. You are hoisting a big red flag at that stage!

The same goes for websites like Oddschecker and gambling forums. These may be sites that some losing punters reside on, just because you've used them already on your device doesn't mean you're doomed. But if the bookies are aware of the other industry sites you're using, it's another red flag against you that you are an organised person who researches heavily what you're doing. Hence why the 2 device setup is so important.

Your required actions
If you're not using two devices yet then it's time to start right now! You also need to clear your cookies immediately from the device you've been using. Get in the habit of using two devices all the time. And have a VPN on your research device for extra protection. Create a folder on your research device if you must to store the blogs/forums/gambling sites you use, if indeed you use any at all.

For calculating odds and Lay bet amounts don't use a website, create yourself a spreadsheet or find a spreadsheet online that you can save. There are a few out there so a quick search of your preferred search engine using your research-only device will turn them up.

Don't join bookies using links on matched betting sites or blogs (if possible)

This ties into the point above. I always clear my cookies to be double sure and then visit a web address directly in my browser. I know if I've clicked on an affiliate link anyway, but it's always good to feel sure. An affiliate link is one that a website owner places to receive commission if you click on it and then signup at the website you've clicked through to. They'll often be long links with lots of digits. Sometimes they are redirected so it looks like you're clicking a link to another page on the same website, but then it redirects you, cheeky little monkeys!

Why shouldn't you join through an affiliate link? This isn't being horrible to stop a website owner making some money in commissions if that's what you're thinking. It's because the bookies have to track each affiliates signups in order to pay them. If an affiliate owns a matched betting website and the bookie sees all their signups come from that website and are all matched bettors, they know a load of accounts to put limits on! Easy pickings.

When you think of it from the bookies point of view – would they rather someone see's a TV advert and goes straight to the website and joins, or someone visits a matched betting website, gets told how to make guaranteed profits, and then signs up. They'll always prefer the first option!

The downside is obviously that the person you learnt information from, or get good tips from, won't get a penny from you not using their affiliate links. What I recommend is you remember the website where you discovered a new bookie, or a website that generally helps you, and then repay them in another way. If they have affiliate links for other stuff like books you could perhaps click on those and buy through those links, or alternatively when you've made some nice profit you could contact them directly and tell them their information has been valuable but you avoided their affiliate links, so can you send them a bit of cash through PayPal, or even a fraction of Bitcoin as a thank you. Obviously this is completely optional but if you make thousands of pounds and certain websites have helped you massively and you're feeling very thankful to those guys and girls who help you out then it can be nice to repay them if you avoided their affiliate links.

Your required actions

If you've already joined through affiliate links then obviously it's too late, there's nothing you can do. I wouldn't go worrying too much though because with all the other tactics listed in this book you still have a good chance of being absolutely fine. But in future, any new sites that you sign-up with, clear your cookies and visit the website directly by typing their web address into the browser address bar. Remember to save how you discovered the bookie site for any future gratuity.

Be aware of companies that are linked

Did you know that in 2016 Betfair and Paddy Power merged together? Then in 2020 they merged again, this time with SkyBet and PokerStars. It created one gigantic gambling company! You know what companies merging together can mean. It can mean sharing resources, sharing staff, and yes, sharing data! Surely this means that they're ability to link your accounts across platforms is significantly easier. This increases the risk of getting gubbed at multiple bookie websites, not just one website. It doesn't mean don't use them, just think about how you might alter your behaviour on the different sites if they're all part of the same group. For example you wouldn't want to put a bet on a football match for the home team to win at Paddy Power and the away team to win at SkyBet.

Your required actions

When joining new websites be sure to do a quick search on the internet to see who owns the website. If it's part of a group that own another site you have an account with, you know to tread lightly and work extra hard to not raise red flags.

Mix up your details

This ties in to the previous point! This is highly unlikely to actually make a difference, but it's yet another tiny confidence booster I like to do so I thought it's worth chucking in. I use a completely different username on each website, I also have a few different email addresses and a few different payment methods. Most banks are free to open accounts so I think it's worth doing. However, don't use credit cards because I found out the hard way the banks will sometimes charge you fees because they class it as a cash withdrawal! I'm told that doesn't apply for all credit cards, but just be aware if you use it then a fee may be charged and it may also affect your credit score. It's better to play it safe and not use credit cards.

For mixing up your details you can also try entering your postcode slightly differently across the websites, for example if you're the Queen (you probably aren't, but if you are then thanks for buying this book Maam!) and joining a website you could type your postcode in as 'SW1A 1AA' or try it lowercase without a space like this; 'sw1a1aa'. You can try changing the formatting of other parts of your address too.

Why bother with this? I feel it's yet another tiny way for accounts to stand less of a chance of being automatically linked by the bookies computer systems as being the same person. Realistically I imagine they put a lot more weight behind things like identical I.P addresses, same first name and surname, checking ID like driving license etc, so will this stop them realising you're a member of multiple bookies running a profitable system? No, not if they're really looking hard enough. But if they're running loose checks using an automated system you may be able to skirt under the radar. Even the postcode may not come up as identical if they require the same upper/lower case and spaces.

On the topic of details I would avoid joining public forums and commenting on public blogs, or Reddit, with the same username you use on bookies sites. There's a fair chance the bookies are monitoring those sites and if you use the same username everywhere they may spot you. If you absolutely feel the need to use these public sites use a completely unrelated username.

Your required actions

Use different usernames, emails and generally mix up details when you can. This is a tip that is certainly not necessary and unlikely to make a big difference, but I like to go the extra mile and leave no stone unturned, that's why I do it. If you're the same way you might want to do it as well as an extra confidence booster.

Delete this spyware from your computer

This section is very important, especially if you're already an established user of a few bookies. If so make sure you do this immediately.

The spyware in question is called 'ieSnare'. It's nothing new and has been around for years, it's one tool the bookies use to spy on gamblers to check the bookies aren't going to be victims of fraud by punters. It makes sense for the bookies to have this sort of protection and on the surface it appears like a good thing for all of us. Nobody wants money launderers and crooks using stolen identities to be all over the bookies. This spyware helps the bookies stay as safe as they can. Unfortunately the bookies appear to have taken it further over time to also spy on those doing arbitrage betting and matched betting. This is why we don't want the 'ieSnare' spyware spying on us!

Rather than putting all the details here it's much better for me to send you to the place I found out about it, I can't take credit for this because I feel lucky to have discovered it! I have nothing to do with the website I'm about to link to, but it's what helped me and so I'm happy to send them a bit of traffic so you can follow their instructions too.

Your required actions

The instructions you need to follow are on this page:
https://www.beatingbetting.co.uk/matched-betting-tips/how-to-block-iesnare/

It's completely free to do, it may take you a few minutes to get your head around it. Read through the instructions a couple of times first before you then follow it. Make sure you get this right because it's very important!

Always place mug bets

What is a 'mug bet'? In the industry it's generally considered a bet that involves no promotion or bonus. But I take it even further than that.

Whatever your broad description of a 'mug bet', the aim is simple, the bets are designed to make you look like a natural punter. I've heard of people doing mug bets in a few different ways. Some match them as closely as possible between bookies to guarantee a tiny loss each time. So if you're betting on football you would bet on the home team to win using one website and Lay them to win at another website. Others do it differently and just earmark small amounts to bet knowing over time it will average out close to break-even if you bet on big favourites, or at least a loss as small as if you'd matched each bet.

Using the second way you may be thinking, "This will definitely lose me money." Have no fear. Over time if you're placing sensible bets, mainly on big favourites, they should only result in a small loss long-term, some will be losers, but most will be winners. Albeit tiny profits because you bet on the favourites. And of course in some months your mug bets will go well and make a clear profit adding to your top line, this can flatter your months effort so make sure you know it's only because of mug bets and will probably swing against you next month.

The reason I go for the second strategy is because accounts can be linked across different bookies (as mentioned earlier in the book). If you're using the first method and the bookies collude to understand lots of different accounts are all controlled by you, then you're in a spot of bother and looking at lots of gubbings. That can't happen with the second method because you're not laying the bet.

Mug bets are very important, never get complacent! Remember to keep them consistent with your matched betting or arbitrage betting patterns as well. They need to be in the same markets (as mentioned earlier, stick to specific markets), with similar stake amounts. It's no good all the bets you are match betting on being at stakes of £10 and £20 and then the mug bets being £0.20 bets on big favorites! If anything that's even more of a red flag.

Mug bets are easy to do, they should be completely normal bets not part of any offers. You should generally place them using your accounts that are nicely in profit. Bookies aren't going to close losing accounts so don't worry about those. Remember these bets can come in and add to our profits too so have a little think about your mug bets and enjoy it.

Your required actions
In your betting logs record mug bets so you can see how many you are placing and keep in the habit of placing enough. You need to be doing them regularly to show normal behaviour. How regular will depend on your overall betting habits, this is a number you'll have to decide on.

Use different areas of bookie sites

Lots of bookies now have more than just betting markets, they have online casinos, bingo areas, arcade games and slots. Using other sections of websites can make you look more natural and may be looked upon more favourably. Each week don't be afraid to use different parts of websites you like, I often use slots on websites where I have a decent sum. I will commit myself to sinking £10 in - which lasts a while at 20p a spin – and call it quits there. I also use the bonuses the bookies offer on their casino games. Often they are things like "wager £50 and get 10 free spins". I often won't even reach near the £50 wager but just by accepting the offer it shows I'm an active casino player. However you definitely don't want to be taking every offer, otherwise once again it highlights you as someone only interested in profiting, as opposed to someone playing for fun.

This also presents the opportunity for a big slice of luck with a decent win. In fact on one Wednesday evening I managed to win a shade over £260 in a couple of hours, I didn't even win a big jackpot, the slots game just kept getting me on the bonus feature even though I was only playing at the minimum of 20p a spin! It added up to a very healthy evening's work! Fair to say I was chuffed and it made for a good month. It was pure luck!

That example is obviously not the norm and you have to anticipate losing, but sometimes you will get good wins. On some of the websites look out for each slot games RTP, it stands for "Return to Player", most will be in the mid to high 90 percents. This means, for example if the RTP is 97%, on average for every £100 you wager you'll get back £97. The small percentage difference is where the house makes it's profits. It may sound like a tiny profit but obviously when you consider the millions that's wagered each day you can see why they make so much juicy profit!

The RTP is why you can be confident over the long-term it shouldn't cost you much. The losses are a small price to pay anyway to make your account look more natural. And the flukes of big wins now and again will make for some stand-out months!

A key warning here is obviously to not be stupid. If you have a very addictive personality then don't do this. If you seriously lack self control also don't do it, just stick to your betting strategy.

Consider the alternatives if things like slots and roulette don't suit your personality, some of the sites have bingo and arcade games which you could try. The key thing is to manage it and don't let it eat noticeably into your profits. Remember the aim is to blend into the crowd and look natural.

Your required actions

Every couple of weeks, set aside a small amount of time to play on other areas of the bookies sites, more so the sites which you are profitable on. Commit an amount to lose and if you reach that amount then stop. The amount to commit should be relative to your situation, if you are a regular money maker who has been doing this for a while you may be happy to commit £15 every couple of weeks to wager. With an RTP in the 90%'s you should get quite a bit of it back. Don't be too robotic on how much you wager because once again it would be a red flag! So vary it. If you're just starting out, set a much lower limit so betting profits aren't eaten into. Remember to make sure this doesn't eat into your profits unnecessarily! We are doing this to look natural, not for a thrill or any other reason.

Go for different odds

When placing bets at each bookie don't always just go with those that are low, like 1.7, 1.8. Really mix it up. Look at your history with each bookie if you have to. Mix it up by placing bets on ones that are 5.2, 7.9 or even as high as 10 or 11. Or as in my golf example earlier in the book, they can be even higher! Do this whether for mug bets or as part of your main betting strategy. If you're matched betting and the bet is matched correctly elsewhere it doesn't matter what odds the bet is!

Your required actions

Be conscious of this and make an effort to mix it up when placing your bets. Go for big underdogs some times, even in mug bets.

Rounded numbers

Don't bet amounts like £12.37 if you're doing matched betting. This is common in matched betting because of the spreadsheet calculators that us matched bettors use. But it looks very suspicious. It's just not natural behaviour to be betting such random amounts every time! It's a fairly easy red flag against you if/when a member of the bookies staff takes a peek in your account and sees loads of random numbers! Round up or down to the pound if you can, or at least a sensible number like £12.50.

The downside of this? It will mean we lose out on a little bit of profit. Qualifying bets may have a slightly bigger loss than we want, and when we take advantage of free bets it may reduce our winnings. Overall if it means losing a little bit each time that's fine, it's a small price to pay for the sake of keeping all our accounts safe and in good standing order for many decades.

Your required actions

If you've already been doing this then don't worry it's not the end of the world because I did it too when I first started and I didn't get gubbed for it. Long-term you need to stop it though. As I've said many times in this book now, put it in your notes or do whatever you have to do to make sure you don't forget this and are always betting rounded amounts.

When depositing don't just deposit the minimum amount

It can be a habit of many matched bettors to only deposit the minimum required. If an offer is 'deposit £20 and get a £20 free bet' many people deposit £20. This can be yet another flag you're someone in it more for the offers than the fun of betting.

To counteract it you should mix up deposit amounts. This doesn't only mean deposit more than you will need, sometimes you could only take advantage of part of an offer. Why not deposit half and only get half the bonus amount? You may not want to do this but on occasions when you're already near your monthly/yearly profit target then it's a good opportunity.

When you deposit more than the value of bonus offers it can also signal an intent to keep betting no matter what, even if you lose at the start, the bookies want people like this meaning it can be a nice green flag our account is a good one for them and certainly not one to be gubbed.

Don't always only deposit when there are bonuses to be had, it looks more natural if you also do deposits when no bonuses are to be had.

Your required actions
Mix up the amounts you deposit, just because the amount needed is £20 to trigger a bonus doesn't mean you have to put that amount in, put in £40 or £50 instead. And don't always do it on offers, do deposits when there are no offers.

Keep money in accounts for as long as possible

The bookies will obviously like you more if you keep money in your betting account. It'll also arouse suspicion if an account is constantly taking money out. Limiting the number of withdrawals you do will help you stay under the radar.

You obviously don't want to go too far with this, it becomes a risk to build up massive accounts with thousands of pounds in. Find a balance, don't let the accounts get too big, but don't constantly take money out.

The challenge is moving your money around. There may be an offer on another site you want to take advantage of but you don't have the cash in your bank account. The temptation is to withdraw £30 from one bookie to deposit it in another, this is where the withdrawals can start to add up though. Always use the cash in your bank as much as possible instead of withdrawing from one to deposit on another bookies website.

Your required actions
Keep a log of your transactions in a spreadsheet (deposits and withdrawals) and you will be able to see the last time you took out money from a bookie and how much it was. It's a quick and easy way to not overdo it.

Profits - keep the long-term in perspective

Smaller in the short-term is better. I genuinely believe that. The bookies have huge databases so they will use automated software to sift through to see which accounts are worth exploring. If you're making £400 per month (which is spread out amongst using many bookies) there's a lot more chance of you slipping under the radar compared to someone making huge sums.

To put it one way. Do you want to make on average £800 per month but for only 5 months? Or on average £300 per month for the next 10 years? The first one totals £4,000 and the second one totals a whopping £36,000. How much money would you prefer to make? And of course these numbers are conservative, full-time gamblers with good systems obviously make colossal amounts more than this over the long-term, but I want to keep the numbers broad and more accurate to amateurs doing it on weekends and evenings.

Your required actions
Set rough targets to keep yourself in check. Write them down. Always keep the long-term in perspective.

Avoid high volume

What's more natural? Someone logging in each day and putting 20 bets on, or someone logging in twice a week and putting only a handful of bets on for fun? We always want to look as natural as possible.

Ultimately, high volume and good profits combine to make a massive red flag on a professional gambler who long-term the bookie will want to limit the damage they take from them!

Of course when lots of opportunities come along you'll be placing plenty of bets. Try your hardest to spread them out between bookies so that for each individual bookie you aren't placing a high volume of bets.

Your required actions

Spread yourself around the different bookies to keep volume low at each bookie. Keep in check monthly profits (talked about in previous point) to help keep volume down.

Concentrate, I'm not kidding!

This may sound dumb but hear me out. This point is worth mentioning for all areas of your betting efforts. Not just to avoid being gubbed. It'll not only affect your profitability but you may also make mistakes that mean you don't put into practice the points explained in this book. Mistakes could lead to a gubbing that could have been avoided!

I've also seen it mentioned plenty of times on forums, and done it twice myself. Mucking up matched bets because of a lack of concentration! It's easy to get complacent after a while and mistakes can creep in. They cost you money though, and mistakes can add up if you keep making them. Always double check your numbers when calculating. If you're someone who sometimes thinks they're a billy big balls who never makes mistakes, you're not, be humble.

Good concentration will mean less chance of being gubbed and better profitability.

Your required actions
Be in a clear mind, and be feeling good enough so that you can concentrate! Otherwise leave the computer alone to come back tomorrow.

Learn from any gubbings

I always keep my expectations in check. I've spent years thinking I'm going to be gubbed and yet I never have been (touch wood!). By presuming that one day I will get at least one gubbing I feel it will soften the blow when it does happen. Instead I plan to use it as an opportunity to learn. If you've already been gubbed at one or two bookies I hope you're using this book to perhaps think of reasons you were gubbed.

Your required actions

If you do receive an email from a bookie saying your account has been limited, come back to this book and read through it again. Think of how they could have known you were a pro operating a system for profit. Learn from it. If needs be make changes to your other bookies accounts, or changes to your routines. This could help avoid more gubbings.

Leave time gaps between new accounts after gubbings

Like I said earlier in the book, I've never experienced a single gubbing as a result of taking the actions mentioned in this book. So this one is a bit of a guess, but I think it makes sense. If you do have an account gubbed it may be best to leave a bit of breathing time before creating a new account on another website. There's a huge amount of bookies websites there's no reason not to have loads of accounts! But if the bookies are sharing data then your details may be passed to other bookies, and that's how the domino effect of more gubbings can happen. For that reason I think it makes sense to maybe have a breather if you get gubbed and not open a new account on another website for a little while.

Your required actions

If you do get gubbed, keep the email informing you of the account limitation/closure. That way you know the date it happened. Then mark on your calendar or somewhere else, a date a few months in the future, probably make it at least 3 months in the future. And only then should you start opening new accounts to replace the gubbed on.

Be straight

This should probably go without saying but I thought I better mention it. Don't start thinking about dodgy activity to try and get ahead. Never register multiple accounts or try and game the systems in any way, the bookies put a lot of money into security because they obviously don't want money launderers or cheats. If a fleeting thought ever even entered your head about registering multiple accounts or anything like that then don't even bother. It's a sure fire way to mess things up and be able to make no money whatsoever!

Your required actions

Don't be an idiot! Keep reminding yourself - choose profits for decades, not weeks!!

A quick case study before my conclusions

By now I hope you've read through all of the points above and absorbed them. To bring it all together I thought I would use a real world example of someone getting banned, and how it could have potentially been avoided with what I've told you in this book.

This is not a perfect example because it's not of someone who did matched betting or arbitrage, but of someone who made money purely on horse racing, but the points here are still valid because the person is a very organised and profitable bettor.

The information I'm using is from a skilled bettor who made money on the horses. It's an article that was published in the Guardian newspaper a while back, in August 2015.

If you would like to read the whole article here's the link, but it's not absolutely critical that you do:
https://www.theguardian.com/global/2015/aug/02/betting-horses-gambling-bookmakers-accounts-closed

Let's crack on with breaking down the interesting points.

Hours looking at horses form

Here is a screenshot of the exact quote in the article:

And I spend a couple of hours every evening after work poring over the horses' form on my computer.

This ties in beautifully with what I said in my tip titled "Use two devices, one for placing bets and one for web research/info". Clearly from what the person has said they did plenty of research. There's a chance the bookies will have seen this from his referral URLs (pages last visited when he landed on the bookies website) and boom, they know what type of punter he is! This could have been avoided with my advice of using two devices. Even if his account was still investigated after the big win there's more chance of them thinking he just got lucky rather than was an expert if he'd have done the two devices trick.

£18,000 profit

Next up is the quote about how much money he made. Here's the screenshot:

> included Pineau de Re, backed at 40-1 for the Crabbie's Grand National. I finished the year exactly £18,012.92 in profit.

This ties in with what I said about "Profits - keep the long-term in perspective". One massive year may well be enough to get you gubbed. You stand a much better chance of being under the radar making much lower profits than that. Plus if you imagine spreading, for example, £6,000 a year profit between 30 bookmakers you're actually only making a small amount at individual bookies, that's £200 per bookie (on average) over an entire year. From the sounds of the article it's likely the £18,000 profit was only spread between a small handful of bookies. We stand a much better chance of avoiding being gubbed then this guy with our tactics of spreading money between bookies and keeping smaller but much longer-term consistent profits.

Other account restrictions followed

Now we have the quote about how more restrictions quickly followed. Here's the screenshot:

> Other account restrictions followed and I was finding it harder and harder to get my bets (typically between £50 and £200) placed with my bookmakers, many of

This ties in to what I said about "Mix up your details" to have a chance of accounts not being linked. It seems clear the bookies have some sort of black list or way of communicating people who have been gubbed. If you can avoid accounts being linked then being gubbed once doesn't mean a domino effect has to happen.

Other notes I want to mention about the article

When you read the article it sounds quite clear he only bet on the horses. Using my advice of, "Use different areas of bookie sites", such as casinos, may have helped his account stay under the radar, or at least give him a brighter future with the bookies.

It sounds like he also only bet on the horses. If you have at least 2 or 3 sports, like I recommended, you stand more chance of looking natural and less like a pro. They may also only restrict on one sport meaning you can still try and make money on others. Although that wouldn't have helped the guy in this article because his only love appeared to be for horses.

Late in the article the guy says the following.

I should point out that not all my bookmakers have turned away my bets. Ladbrokes and bet365 have invariably been willing to lay me a fair-size wager, but they are in the minority.

This shows that even if you do get gubbed at some accounts, it doesn't mean all will massively restrict you meaning some money can still be made. This should offer encouragement if you've read this book and are in fear of being gubbed because of certain things it's too late to change. Remember this is a guy who banked 18K profit in one year and had done lots of things to give the bookies red flags he's a pro, and yet he can still go placing decent sized bets at sites like Ladbrokes and Bet365!

Case study conclusion

I hope this real world example shows you how putting into action the advice I've given in this book can significantly help you lower your chances of being gubbed.

If you want to find more examples of people being gubbed I recommend you do some Google searches and look at popular gambling forums and other forums like MoneySavingExpert. I warn you though that you will find many people who've been gubbed (recommend this book to them please ha!), at first that may seem scary, but if you look deep in their reasons why they think it happened, you can also see how this book could have saved them! Remember though the "Two devices" advice earlier, don't do the researching on the device you will be using to bet on!!

Book conclusions

First off congratulations for getting this far and making your way through the book! I'm very confident it will pay off for you (provided you actually follow everything you've just read!). The fact you've got this far shows you are keen to make a success of your betting endeavours, that is why I have confidence in you.

Nobody can predict the future. Who knows what will change in the future, maybe the bookies get super powers to track down every matched bettor and arbitrager and close their accounts! Fair to say that is insanely unlikely though. I also never believe it when people say "if you make a profit they will close your account eventually". The bookies need winning players! They're the ones that tell all their friends about the site they use for their winnings. Plus if they just closed the account of every player that was a winner then everyone would realise that eventually and their reputations would be in tatters and nobody would bother! So don't have any fear about sustainability if you follow this book.

All these things pointed out in this book mean I look forward to making lots more money, every single month, for a long time to come! Provided you make the effort and put into action pointers made above, you too should also look forward to smiling at your spreadsheet each month when you tot up the profits made!

I would say good luck to end this book. However you don't need luck, you need to put in the effort and you will get the justified rewards for many years and decades! So go ahead and do it now!

Thanks for reading. Dillon Bleakley.

Printed in Great Britain
by Amazon

81367362R00031